SUPERSTITIONS SURROUNDING

LUCKY NUMBERS

Tammy Gagne

Stride
An Imprint of The Child's World®
childsworld.com

The Child's World
childsworld.com

Published by The Child's World®
800-599-READ • childsworld.com

Photography Credits
Photographs ©: Selena May/Shutterstock Images, cover (numbers 4 and 7), 1 (numbers 4 and 7); Perepadia Y./Shutterstock Images, cover (numbers 3, 8, 9, and 12), 1 (numbers 3, 8, 9, and 12); Shutterstock Images, 5; Roberto David/iStockphoto, 6; Oleg Golovnev/Shutterstock Images, 9; Zhang Meng/iStockphoto, 11; Sean Pavone/Shutterstock Images, 12; Sarawut Sukasem/Shutterstock Images, 15; Renata Sedmakova/Shutterstock Images, 16; Arie Rinanda/Shutterstock Images, 19; Evrim Ertik/iStockphoto, 21

ISBN Information
9781503865082 (Reinforced Library Binding)
9781503866461 (Portable Document Format)
9781503867307 (Online Multi-user eBook)
9781503868144 (Electronic Publication)

LCCN 2022939521

Printed in the United States of America

BRINGING THE WORLD 19 68 TO YOUNG READERS

About the Author

Tammy Gagne has written hundreds of books for both adults and children. Some of her recent books have been about desert ecosystems and space tourism. She lives in northern New England with her husband, son, and dogs.

CONTENTS

CHAPTER ONE

LOTS OF LUCK

Some of the most popular **superstitions** are related to numbers. From ancient times, people used numbers to make sense of the world. Eventually, people started to believe that certain numbers were either lucky or unlucky.

Fortune cookies often include lucky numbers. Some people buy lottery tickets based on the numbers they receive in these fun treats.

Many people attach meanings to certain numbers. This might make them think the numbers are lucky or unlucky.

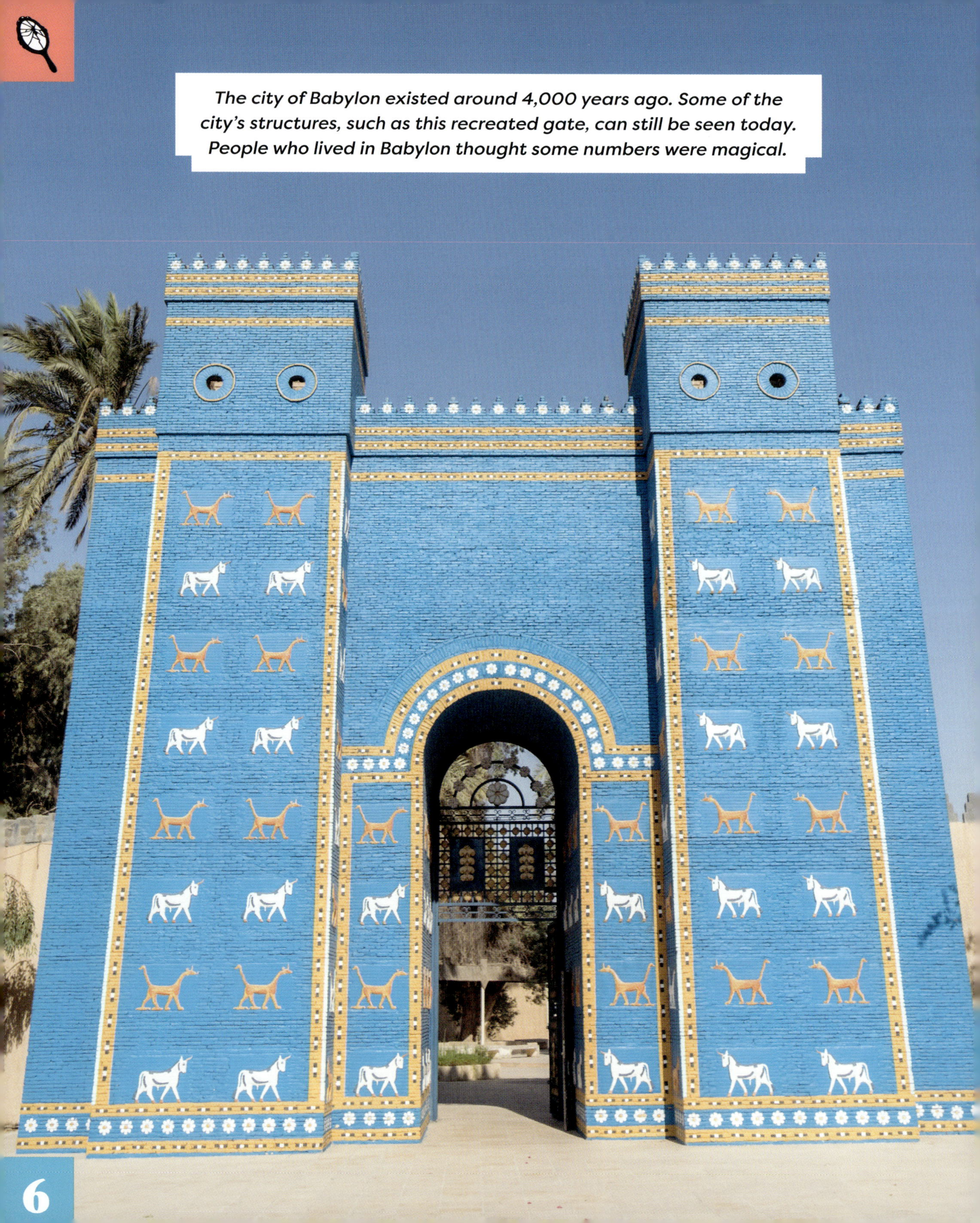

The city of Babylon existed around 4,000 years ago. Some of the city's structures, such as this recreated gate, can still be seen today. People who lived in Babylon thought some numbers were magical.

Many ancient **civilizations** used numbers to predict, or tell the future of, events in nature and astronomy. Astronomy is the study of things in the universe, such as the stars and planets. The ancient Egyptians used numbers to figure out when the Nile River would flood. The Babylonians watched how planets moved. They noted the times and distances. They then used this information to predict **eclipses**. Early scientists used math for calculation, but others based religions around numbers. The Greeks even had a **cult** that believed numbers ruled the entire universe.

The superstition that numbers can affect luck is the basis of numerology. Numerology is the study of numbers that looks at dates of birth and the number of letters in names. Numerologists believe that these and other numbers define a person's strengths, challenges, and personality. Numerologists even think numbers predict a person's future, much like **horoscopes**.

Some people believe that certain numbers bring good fortune to everyone. Others think they have lucky numbers of their own. They may see a date as lucky because something good happened to them on that day. People often look for these numbers in everyday life, hoping that they will bring them more luck.

Some people look forward to certain dates. They connect these dates with good things.

CHAPTER TWO

ODD NUMBERS

There are many superstitions about numbers in Chinese **culture**. It is common for people in China to plan important events on dates they consider lucky. For example, the number nine in Mandarin Chinese sounds like another word meaning "long-lasting." A wedding held on a date ending in nine is thought to lead to a long marriage.

Numerologists say the age 21 is lucky, but they call 63 unlucky. However, becoming 64 is said to bring good luck. This superstition states that living past 63 means a person will live many years longer.

Holding a wedding on a lucky date is important in Chinese culture.

In Japanese, the number nine is pronounced "ku," which sounds like the word for suffering or torture.

Superstitions about numbers are also found in other countries. Language often links numbers to words with similar meanings. For example, in Japan the number nine is seen as bad luck. This is because the Japanese word for that number sounds like another word that means "suffering."

People in many cultures see the number seven as lucky. The Christian Bible offers one explanation. The text states that God created the world in six days and took the seventh day to rest. For this reason, some Christians see the number seven as a symbol of completeness.

The number three is also seen as lucky by many Christians. That is because of the religion's belief in the Holy Trinity, which is made up of God, Jesus, and the Holy Spirit. Other religions also place great value on this number. Hinduism has its own trinity, or a group of three gods, in the gods Brahma, Vishnu, and Shiva. The number three is also important in Islam because of its three holy sites: Mecca, Medina, and Jerusalem.

The number three is considered holy in Hinduism because it represents Brahma, Vishnu, and Shiva.

Judas was the 13th guest at the Last Supper, a final meal Jesus had with his disciples.

Odd numbers are generally associated with good luck. But bad luck is linked to some odd numbers, too. For example, not all people like the number three. They believe that bad things happen in threes. The number 13 is also said to bring bad luck. Christians relate this number to Judas. He was the 13th guest at an important dinner Jesus attended. Judas betrayed Jesus soon after this event.

CHAPTER THREE

EVEN NUMBERS

Even lucky numbers are just as popular as odd lucky numbers. For example, people in some Western cultures think the number four is lucky. This may be because so many things in nature occur in groups of four. Earth, air, fire, and water are often called the four elements of life. There are also four seasons on Earth.

People in Eastern cultures do not see this number as lucky, though. Traditions in China, Japan, Korea, and Vietnam have linked the number to bad luck. This is because the word for the number four sounds like the word for death in these languages.

Even numbers, like the number four, are considered lucky in some countries.

Many Chinese people think the number eight is the luckiest number. They see it as a symbol of wealth. Again, the sound of the word has a lot to do with this superstition. The Mandarin word for the number eight sounds much like the word that means "to get rich."

Sometimes much larger numbers are linked to luck. This is the case with 786. People throughout India see this number as lucky or holy.

Some people in China change their phone numbers to include the number eight. People may even buy a house with this number in the address because they think it will bring them good fortune.

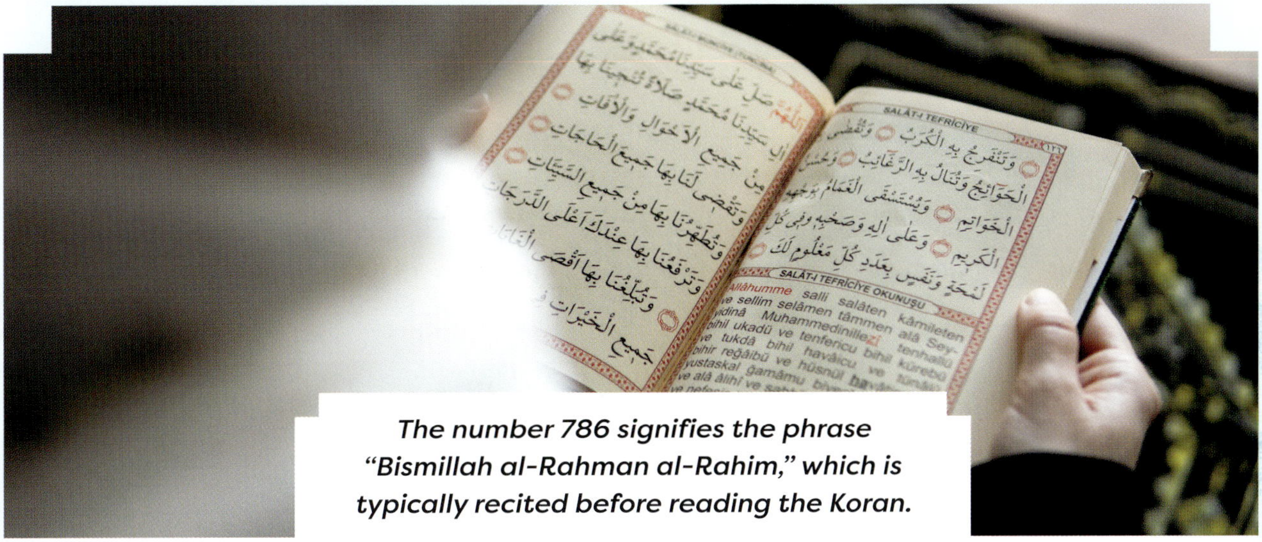

The number 786 signifies the phrase "Bismillah al-Rahman al-Rahim," which is typically recited before reading the Koran.

The number 786 is related to the Islamic sacred book called the Koran. Some Muslims even use the number as another term for Allah, the Muslim name for God. They often say the number before starting an important task. In Burma, people often display this number in their homes or shops. They believe it brings them Allah's blessing. Many Hindus also view 786 as lucky and holy.

There is no evidence that shows numbers can bring a person good or bad luck. But many people around the world still believe in the power of numbers. Others simply enjoy learning about the different cultural meanings behind certain numbers.

GLOSSARY

civilizations (sih-vuh-luh-ZAY-shunz) Civilizations are well-developed societies with specific cultures and traditions. Ancient Egypt was one of the most powerful ancient civilizations.

cult (KUHLT) A cult is a group of people brought together by shared devotion to a particular belief. A cult in ancient Greece thought numbers controlled the universe.

culture (KUHL-chur) The ways of life, customs, ideas, and traditions that a group of people hold is known as their culture. Chinese culture has some superstitions about numbers.

eclipses (eh-KLIP-suhz) Eclipses happen when the moon, Earth, and sun line up, blocking all or part of the sun's light. The Babylonians predicted eclipses using numbers.

horoscopes (HAWR-uh-skohps) Horoscopes are predictions of future events based on the arrangement of planets, stars, and other celestial bodies at a person's birth. Horoscopes often tell people when good luck or misfortune is on the way.

superstitions (soo-pur-STIH-shuhnz) Superstitions are beliefs that certain events, objects, or numbers cause good or bad luck. Believing in lucky numbers is one of the many superstitions that exist.

FAST FACTS

- A superstition is a belief that certain things can trigger either good or bad luck. Many superstitions involve numbers.
- Numerology is based on the belief that certain numbers can predict the future.
- Many superstitions about numbers come from religions.
- Some number superstitions came about because the numbers sound similar to certain words or phrases in different languages.

ONE STRIDE FURTHER

- Do you have a lucky number? Why did you decide it was lucky for you?
- Do you believe that certain numbers can bring good or bad luck? Why or why not?
- Why do you think that so many cultures around the world believe in the power of numbers?

FIND OUT MORE

IN THE LIBRARY

Gagne, Tammy. *Friday the 13th*. Parker, CO: The Child's World, 2023.

Layton, Christine. *Travel to China*. Minneapolis, MN: Lerner, 2022.

Syed, Tayyaba. *Islam*. New York, NY: Britannica Educational Publishing, 2019.

ON THE WEB

Visit our website for links about lucky numbers:
childsworld.com/links

Note to Parents, Teachers, and Librarians: We routinely verify our Web links to make sure they are safe and active sites. So encourage your readers to check them out!

INDEX